The Library of
Future Weather and Climate

Forecasting the Climate of the Future

Paul Stein

 The Rosen Publishing Group, Inc.
New York

Published in 2001 by The Rosen Publishing Group, Inc.
29 East 21st Street, New York, NY 10010

Copyright © 2001 by The Rosen Publishing Group, Inc.

First Edition

Library of Congress Cataloging-in-Publication Data

Stein, Paul, 1968–
Forecasting the climate of the future / Paul Stein.— 1st ed.
p. cm. — (The library of future weather and climate)
Includes bibliographical references and index.
ISBN 0-8239-3413-6 (lib. bdg.)
1. Climatic changes—Computer simulation—Juvenile literature.
[1. Climatic changes—Computer simulation. 2. Nature—Effect of human beings on.] I. Title. II. Series.
QC981.8.C5 S735 2001
551.5'253'0113—dc21

00-011542

All temperatures in this book are in degrees Fahrenheit, except where specifically noted. To convert to degrees Celsius, or centigrade, use the following formula:

Celsius temperature = (5 ÷ 9) x (the temperature in Fahrenheit - 32)

Manufactured in the United States of America

Contents

Introduction

The year is 2100. The location is Fairbanks, Alaska. It's spring, and central Alaska once again emerges from the darkness and cold of winter. Fairbanks has always been known for its frigid winters, but things have changed over the decades. Now it just doesn't get as cold as it used to. Winter temperatures still fall below zero, but the old-timers remember when temperatures of 50 below were not uncommon. Now that kind of bitter cold hardly ever occurs. During the late twentieth century, ice on the local rivers would begin to break apart and melt during the first week of May. Now warm springtime air and sunshine clear the rivers of ice in early April. Snow, as always, lies in leftover heaps, the melting remains of the hundred inches that commonly fall each winter—nearly thirty

Global warming may one day mute the brilliant displays of fall foliage in New England.

more inches per year than used to fall, on average, around the year 2000. Outside of town, acres of gray, splintered tree trunks mark the locations of long dead forests, victims of heavy, branch-breaking winter snow, summer insects, and soggy, sinking land.

As spring turns into summer in the year 2100, residents of Dallas, Texas, prepare for the coming months of blazing heat, dust storms, and lack of rain. Heat was always part of summer life in Dallas, but now summers start earlier and last longer, and are just plain hotter. Most days, the temperature soars above 100 degrees, sometimes even over 110. At night, temperatures often refuse to dip below 80 degrees. Whereas in June, July, and August, rainfall used to tally over half a foot back around the turn of the century, now summer rainfall is rare.

Weeks go by without a drop. Many farmers have long since migrated away from the north Texas area or turned to new work, forced out by year after year of withering drought. Dust storms, once a rarity in Dallas, are now common, blowing into the city from the abandoned, desolate farm and pasture land to the west of town. Over the years, water has become scarce, despite an abundance of artificial reservoirs built around the city back in the twentieth century. Now there's just not enough rain to keep them all filled.

It's autumn in Burlington, Vermont, and summerlike weather lingers through September and into October. The first killing freeze now doesn't usually occur until late October, and sometimes even early November, a full month later than it used to. To farmers and gardeners, the longer growing season is a delight. To others, however, it just doesn't seem like a New England autumn anymore. The brilliant displays of fall foliage have become more muted over the years and occur later in the season. The first snowflakes don't arrive until late November, whereas back around the year 2000 Burlington residents would usually see some snow in October. In fact, winters in New England are much less white than they used to be. Snowfall used to add up to well over fifty inches per year in Burlington. Now it's a snowy winter if thirty inches fall. Some of the nearby ski areas have closed, and others have shortened their season. White Christmases are a rare treat.

It's winter in Los Angeles. As the year 2100 turns into 2101, Los Angeles residents brace for another round of punishing Pacific storms. Coastal residents board up windows and build walls of sandbags, or hire trucks and bulldozers to move giant rocks into place to break up the crashing waves. Through the decades of the twenty-first century, hundreds of beachfront houses crumbled under the relentless attack of pounding wintertime surf. Rising ocean levels have made the problem even worse, as waves and tides combine to wash away the protective strip of sandy beach. As the winter storms begin to drench the region, torrential rain once again falls on the hills and mountains surrounding the city. Winter rainfall used to be measured in inches, but now it's usually measured by the foot. Mudslides come crashing down valleys, bursting into hillside homes and burying roads. Flooded city streets and highways bring the normally slow flow of traffic to a near dead stop. Winter used to be a time of sunshine and pleasant temperatures, with only occasional rainstorms. Now, the rainy season is something to be feared.

What has happened to our climate? This imaginary picture of future weather across North America in the year 2100 is based on recent predictions made by scientists studying the phenomenon of global warming. Global warming is the rise in average temperature of the earth's atmosphere that has been observed over the last century, especially in the last twenty years. Most scientists think it is caused in large part by the increasing amounts of certain kinds of gases in our atmosphere. These gases, called greenhouse gases, are mainly produced by the burning of fossil fuels like coal, oil, and natural gas. The more fossil fuels that are burned in power plants or in vehicles, the more greenhouse gases enter the atmosphere and the warmer the planet becomes. A warmer planet means changes in climate and weather.

In order to help governments prepare for the effects of global warming over the next century, scientists must try to predict the weather twenty, fifty, even a hundred years ahead. How exactly will rising levels of greenhouse gases in the atmosphere influence climate in the twenty-first century? If greenhouse gases continue to increase at their current rate, how fast will the average temperature of the earth rise? This book discusses how scientists make these long-range climate predictions, the limitations of their tools, and their best guesses so far. Forecasting for the future is a scientific challenge of great complexity and urgency. Knowing even a little about how we may be disturbing the atmosphere and the effects of our actions, we may be in a better position to alter the outcome of events.

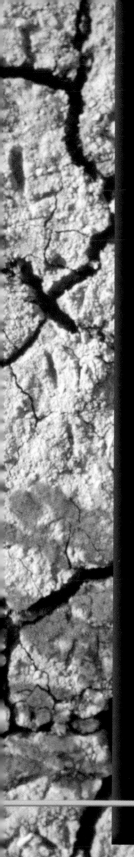

1 The Forecasting Challenge

If the current warming trend in the earth's atmosphere continues, we may be in for some nasty consequences. Rising sea levels could flood low-lying coastal areas and worsen the destructive effects of coastal storms. Drought may wither crops and evaporate drinking water supplies in some areas, while other locations experience more frequent floods. Changing climate may disrupt biomes, causing some species of plants and animals to migrate to new regions or dwindle in number.

Because of these potentially damaging consequences, government officials and scientists are beginning to consider ways to lessen the possible future threat. Most agree that the best way to reduce our disruptive impact on climate would be to develop alternate sources of energy and decrease the amount of green-house gases getting pumped into the atmosphere. However, this would be a difficult and time-consuming task, requiring cooperation between governments and industry on a global scale. To make matters trickier, scientists are still unsure just how the earth's climate will change in the decades to come. Despite growing evidence, some scientists and government officials remain skeptical that greenhouse gases are contributing to global warming.

So the question is, do we do nothing now and wait to see what happens? Should our present uncertainty about the future of our climate be reason enough to postpone action? While members of government and industry debate this issue, scientists are trying to increase their skill in predicting just how the earth's climate may react to increasing amounts of greenhouse gases. The more accurate these predictions can be, the more confident we may become that the earth's climate is indeed changing, and the more quickly we may be able to act.

To meet this challenge, scientists use powerful supercomputers that predict how rising levels of greenhouse gases may affect the earth's climate. Supercomputers look quite different from ordinary desktop computers. They are very large, sometimes the size of a refrigerator or even bigger, extremely fast, and very expensive. Because they are so expensive, only large companies, universities, and governments own and operate them. Just like regular desktop computers, supercomputers can be used for a variety of purposes. But because they're so powerful, they're ideally suited to run software that simulates the earth's extremely complex natural processes. This kind of software is known to scientists as a model because it models, or simulates, different kinds of natural phenomena. A model that simulates the climate of the earth is called a climate model.

The job of a climate model is to predict how the earth's climate will react to increasing amounts of greenhouse gases. But the task is much more difficult than it may sound. To forecast how the earth's climate may change in the future, climate models

With supercomputers like this one, scientists try to predict the effect of rising levels of greenhouse gases on the earth's climate.

must simulate the variety of natural processes that affect the earth's atmosphere. And there are many of these natural processes, none of which are fully understood by scientists.

To start with, global climate models must be programmed to represent how the temperature of the atmosphere changes. This requires an understanding of the earth's radiation cycle. Radiation is energy in the form of invisible electromagnetic waves that travel at the speed of light. All objects both give off and absorb radiation in different amounts. If an object absorbs more radiation than it emits, it warms. If it emits more radiation than it absorbs, the object cools. And so it is with the earth and its atmosphere. The exchange of radiation between the Sun, the earth, and its atmosphere determines the over-all temperature of the earth.

One of the more important factors that affects how the earth warms or cools over longer periods of time is the amount of carbon dioxide in the atmosphere. Carbon dioxide is one of the most important greenhouse gases because it is a very efficient absorber of the radiation that's given off by the earth. The more carbon dioxide in the atmosphere, the more outgoing radiation is absorbed and the warmer the planet becomes.

The amount of carbon dioxide in the atmosphere is regulated by complicated processes. Humans influence the amount of carbon dioxide in the air by burning fossil fuels. Scientists who program climate models must estimate, based on current trends, just how much more carbon dioxide and other greenhouse gases will be released into the atmosphere in the future. This depends on things like the rate of world population growth, how people consume energy, and whether any action is taken to develop sources of energy other than fossil fuels.

Carbon dioxide is also regulated by natural processes that involve plants and the oceans—processes that can slowly change over time. Oceans absorb carbon dioxide from the atmosphere and return some

Scientists and the automobile industry are searching for alternative ways of powering automobiles because the gas we burn when we drive increases the amount of carbon dioxide in the atmosphere.

of the carbon to the earth's crust in a process that occurs over thousands of years. Plants, on the other hand, regulate atmospheric carbon dioxide over much shorter timescales by absorbing carbon dioxide from the atmosphere. But when plants and trees die, or are cut down by humans, some of this carbon dioxide gets released back into the atmosphere. Climate models, therefore, must simulate how oceans and plants affect carbon dioxide levels.

Oceans not only act to regulate the amount of carbon dioxide in the air but also play a direct role in shaping the earth's climate. Ocean currents such as the Gulf Stream carry warm water away from the Tropics and cold water away from the poles. In this way, they act to

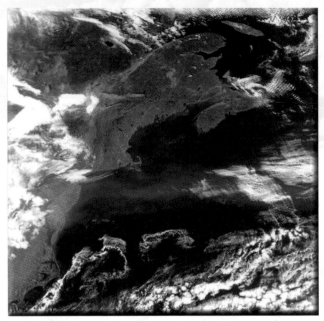

The Gulf Stream helps to regulate heat across the earth by carrying warm water away from the Tropics.

redistribute heat across the planet, preventing heat from building up in tropical regions and preventing polar regions from becoming too cold. The atmosphere above these large, slow-moving currents warms or cools in response to the water below, thereby affecting the earth's climate. And not only does the atmosphere warm and cool in response to the water below it, but the oceans warm or cool in response to the air above. Oceans only slowly absorb heat from the air, however, so ocean water temperatures change much more slowly than air temperatures. It's this two-way interaction between the oceans and the atmosphere that poses such a difficult challenge for climate models.

Not only must global climate models represent how the oceans influence the atmosphere, but also how the land influences the atmosphere. Unlike the oceans, the earth's land surface changes extremely slowly in geological processes that occur over hundreds or thousands of years. What is important as far as climate models are concerned is how the elevation of the land varies over the earth. Large mountain ranges, such as the Rocky Mountains in North

America and the Himalayas in Asia, have a direct influence on global weather patterns. Storm systems and wind currents are deflected in predictable ways by these land features. The more detail in the representation of the land in a climate model, the more realistic the prediction of climate will be.

In the atmosphere itself, clouds are an extremely important part of the climate puzzle. Scientists have learned that the way clouds affect climate depends on their height and thickness. Thin, high clouds are thought to cause warming of the atmosphere as they absorb outgoing radiation emitted by the earth and let through incoming radiation emitted by the Sun. Thick, low clouds, on the other hand, may have a cooling effect as they block sunlight from reaching the earth's surface. But some of this cooling by thick, low clouds may be offset by the warming that occurs when a cloud forms. When clouds form, they release heat into the atmosphere through the process of condensation, whereby invisible, gaseous water vapor in the air turns into tiny cloud droplets. Likewise, the disappearance of clouds, through the process of evaporation, removes heat from the atmosphere as tiny cloud droplets in the air turn back into invisible, gaseous water vapor. Scientists must program climate models to estimate, as accurately as possible, just how the formation and decay of clouds, along with their height and thickness, will act to influence the temperature of the atmosphere.

Ice influences climate in much the same way clouds do. Ice and snow, owing to their bright white color, reflect incoming sunlight

A temperature inversion traps pollutants and toxic gases over Los Angeles. With a warmer climate, there will be more days like this one.

back into space. The more ice and snow there is around the earth, and especially in the polar regions, the more sunlight gets reflected away from the earth and the cooler the earth will be. However, the more the planet warms, the more snow and ice melts. The less ice and snow there is, the less sunlight gets reflected away from the earth and the warmer the earth may become. The role of the polar ice caps offers yet another challenge to the predictive powers of climate models.

The role that humans play in altering the earth's climate is even more complicated. Humans release carbon dioxide and other green-house gases into the atmosphere, leading to a warming of the planet. But industrial emissions also lead to the formation of tiny airborne particles called aerosols. Aerosols range in diameter from 0.001 to 0.01 millimeters and are thought to have a cooling effect on the atmosphere by reflecting incoming sunlight back into space. Unlike carbon dioxide, the amount of aerosols in the air varies considerably around the world. Regions close to heavy industry usually have the highest amounts of aerosols in the air, while remote locations, such as the Sahara Desert or Amazon jungle, typically have low amounts. Aerosols, therefore, can at least partially offset the amount of warming caused by greenhouse gases in certain regions of the world. Climate models must take this into account.

Radiation, carbon dioxide, plants, oceans, mountain ranges, ice caps, aerosols, clouds: The earth's climate is made up of a tangle of different natural processes. The interaction of these forces is extremely complex and not fully understood by scientists. Even the most powerful computer on the planet is not able to simulate the big picture with complete accuracy. Yet climate models must calculate how these phenomena will change over years and decades into the future. The task of predicting the earth's climate, therefore, might appear to be overwhelming. How do scientists do it? How do they program supercomputer climate models to give reliable predictions on the state of our planet decades into the future?

2 Computing the Future Climate

The future has always been shrouded in mystery. Who will win the World Series next year? What presents will I get for my birthday next week? In a hundred years, will people be living on the moon? It's impossible for us to know the answers to these questions. We do know what happened yesterday, or a week ago. We live in the present and are able to reach back into the past. But the future remains hidden in a great cloud of unknowing.

Amazingly, however, science offers a way to predict the future. The person who first discovered this remarkable method was Sir Isaac Newton, a British physicist and mathematician, in the mid-1660s. During those years, Newton invented a new kind of mathematics to describe how objects move. A famous story relates how Newton was

The mathematical equations that Sir Isaac Newton created in the seventeenth century form the basis of how scientists predict the weather today.

struck by a flash of insight as he sat in his orchard one day. Watching an apple fall from a tree, Newton suddenly understood that the movement of the apple toward the earth was governed by a force, which he called gravity. Newton developed the basic mathematical equations that could describe, or predict, how objects move under the force of gravity. For Newton, the world was governed by discoverable forces, and mathematical equations could describe precisely how those forces would behave.

In the following centuries, other mathematicians and scientists developed and extended Newton's basic equations. In theory, these equations could be used to describe how any object moves, from falling apples to the movement of the Moon around the earth and the planets around the Sun. In the 1800s, other equations were developed that described how heat moved within fluids like air and water.

In the early part of the twentieth century, another British mathematician became interested in how all these equations could be used to predict the weather. Lewis Fry Richardson reasoned that since air molecules are objects just like any other object, especially when you consider how lots of them move around together, the movement of air should obey the same physical laws that Newton had discovered over 200 years earlier. The newer equations that described how heat behaves in fluids could be used to predict how air temperatures change. And since scientists could mathematically relate air temperature to air pressure and density, Richardson thought there should in theory be a way to use mathematics to predict the behavior of the atmosphere in the future.

Richardson decided to try to predict the weather over Europe. In order for the equations to work, he needed to know what the weather was at a given point in time. Using these initial conditions, he could then calculate the movement of air and the changes in pressure and temperature that would occur in the future. In the early part of the twentieth century, however, getting a set of initial weather conditions was a difficult task. Unlike today, there was no established network of weather reporting sites around the world. Weather observations were taken somewhat randomly, at relatively few locations, whenever the need arose. However, Richardson was in luck. On May 20, 1910, an unusually complete set of weather observations was recorded for an international balloon festival held in Europe. Richardson had the data he needed.

Richardson then set out to develop a method of calculation. He realized that he would have to take some shortcuts because his set of initial data described only the weather conditions at scattered points around Europe. He had no idea what the weather was doing in the thousands of square miles in between his recording sites. Richardson

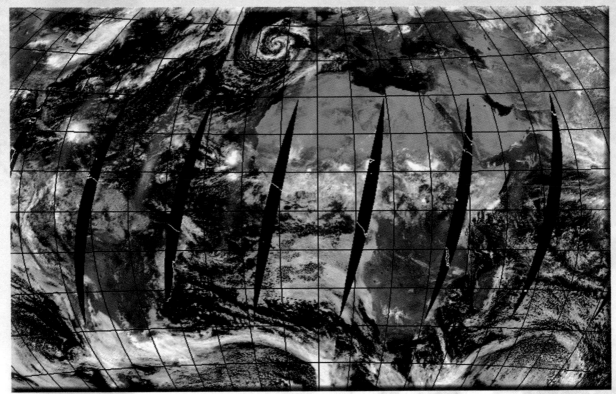

Lewis Fry Richardson's idea of dividing geographical areas into grids has become the standard in modern weather forecasting based on computer modeling.

knew that to get a perfectly accurate mathematical prediction of future weather, he would have to know the movement of every air molecule over Europe, and the pressure and temperature of every square inch of atmosphere. Obviously, this was impossible. There was no way to know the exact movement of every air molecule over Europe, and even if there were, it would take centuries to calculate how the many billions of molecules would move.

Richardson therefore divided a section of Europe into a checkerboard pattern, or grid. The points at the corners of each square in the grid would be the locations where he had accurate weather data. The resolution of Richardson's grid, meaning the distance between each point, was large. Without a fine, detailed grid resolution, Richardson knew that his predictions would be only rough guesses. While he didn't know what the weather was doing in between the grid points, he hoped it was similar to what was observed at the grid points.

Richardson used the initial conditions as input for his equations and then solved them for a small amount of time into the future. Then he took these numbers and reinserted them back into the equations, solving them again and generating different numbers that represented the state of the atmosphere a bit farther into the future. He did this over and over again. Since the equations he used were so difficult and complex, they took a lot of time to solve. In fact, it took Richardson six weeks to calculate a six-hour change in pressure, temperature, and wind over Europe.

The results were discouraging. Richardson's method predicted an extraordinarily large change in air pressure—almost 50 percent larger, in fact, than air pressure is observed to vary over the entire earth. Even so, Richardson and other scientists of the time knew he was on to something. The problems in Richardson's time were three-fold. First, it took far too long for a human to work the calculations. Second, there were not enough weather observations to give a reliable set of initial conditions to use as input for the equations. And third, the equations still did not do a satisfactory enough job in describing how the atmosphere behaved.

Richardson was ahead of his time. The solution to his problems came decades later, in the form of a worldwide network of weather observing stations, new and more detailed mathematical descriptions of the behavior of the air, and, of course, the development of computers.

The computer is the ultimate tool for crunching numbers. What took Richardson six weeks to solve in the second decade of the twentieth century would take a modern computer seconds. In the United States in the 1950s, a new group of scientists realized the potential for using computers to solve the equations that describe atmospheric motions. Computerized models of the atmosphere became gradually more complex and powerful through the 1960s, 1970s, and 1980s. By the 1990s, state-of-the-art supercomputers were doing millions of calculations per second, using thousands of weather observations from around the world and cutting-edge mathematics to predict the weather around the planet days into the future with remarkable accuracy. These computer models use essentially the same methods that Lewis Fry Richardson used over eighty years ago. Taking a set of initial weather conditions as input, they run this data through various equations that mathematically describe the behavior of the atmosphere. Then they take the output from the first run-through and plug it back into the equations, generating a new set of data. Each time the computer solves the equations, it generates numbers that represent the state of the atmosphere slightly farther out in time. Like Richardson, the supercomputers predict weather on a set of grid points laid out over an imaginary, simulated Earth. Typically, these kinds of models forecast short-range weather conditions over specific regions of the world, anywhere from two to ten days in advance.

Climate models developed from short-range weather models work in basically the same way. Short-range models forecast weather over countries, or continents, for days ahead in time. Climate models, however, forecast the weather around the entire planet for decades, or even a century, into the future. They differ from short-range weather models in that they are, by necessity, less detailed. While modern-day supercomputers are lightning-fast, there's still a limit on how much data they can process in a given time period. In order to crunch all the numbers to predict global climate so far out into the future, and to do it in a reasonable amount of time, climate models must be simpler and streamlined.

Even modern climate models running on supercomputers must take shortcuts and make approximations. Powerful as they may be, they still can't predict the motion of every single air molecule around the earth decades ahead. In the next chapter, we'll discuss the various ways that climate models deal with this problem. Even supercomputers have their limits.

3 The Limits of Computer Models

Imagine you're cooking a complicated dinner. You've picked out a recipe that looks interesting. As you begin, however, you feel a bit overwhelmed. Looking at the cookbook, the recipe appears quite complicated, with many different ingredients, including some spices and vegetables that you've never even heard of before. The step-by-step instructions are long and detailed.

As you proceed, you decide to make things a little easier on yourself. Where the cookbook says to bake at 350 degrees for fifty minutes, you decide to save some time and bake at 450 degrees for twenty-five minutes. Where the recipe calls for twenty different kinds of spices, all with different and exacting measurements in teaspoons and tablespoons, you decide to substitute

Television weather reporters get their information almost exclusively from weather centers that predict the weather using supercomputers.

just a couple of spices. And when you go to the pantry to get some garlic, you find that you're all out! Perhaps the meal will taste just as good without it; after all, you're not very fond of garlic anyway.

Baking at a higher temperature for a shorter period of time sounds like it should work, but you find that the food turns out still rather cold on the inside. If you choose the right two spices, the dinner still might turn out well enough, but it certainly won't taste like it would if you used all twenty. Likewise with leaving out the garlic: You still have an edible meal, but it lacks the flavor it would have had otherwise.

Forecasting climate using a computer is like cooking a meal. The workings of the atmosphere are like an incredibly detailed and complex recipe. Climate depends on clouds, polar ice, plants, atmospheric gases, radiation, and a variety of other phenomena. Computers must therefore use shortcuts and substitutions to handle everything in an efficient way. Powerful as they are, they just don't have the ability to calculate the vast workings of the earth with extreme detail. The benefit of making substitutions and approximations is a savings in time. However, just as making shortcuts in cooking makes the meal less tasty, making shortcuts when modeling climate reduces the model's accuracy. But shortcuts are necessary when modeling climate, for a couple of reasons.

To start with, the equations that scientists program into climate models do not represent how the atmosphere works with complete accuracy. Scientists still don't know exactly how many of the natural processes work in the atmosphere and oceans. The equations that describe these natural processes, therefore, make approximations about the way climate behaves in certain situations. These guesses do a good enough job in simulating the way the atmosphere works, but they leave out some details. Scientists must compromise like this to limit the complexity of a model. The more complex the model, the longer it takes to calculate a forecast.

Another way that the model takes shortcuts is by representing certain complicated natural processes, like the formation of clouds, with just a few numbers. This is called parameterization. The formation of clouds is a very complex event, involving the movement of heat and moisture between the earth, the oceans, and the atmosphere. It involves the processes of condensation and evaporation. These processes, in turn, depend on things like air temperature and humidity. Cloud formation also depends on the way the temperature of the atmosphere changes with increasing altitude. Evaporation, condensation, air temperature and humidity, and a host of other natural phenomena result in the formation of different kinds of clouds at varying altitudes in the sky.

For climate models, this is all too much. To represent how clouds form using such detail would be an extremely time-consuming process. Most of the resources of the computer would be taken up just for this task alone, leaving little or nothing for all the rest of the natural phenomena that must be calculated in a climate model.

Pictured here is Hurricane Alberto in August 2000. It is easier for forecasters to predict when a hurricane will form than to tell where it will hit.

The formation of clouds is a complicated natural process that involves the movement of heat and moisture between the earth, the oceans, and the atmosphere.

So, like using two spices for twenty in a recipe, climate models use parameterization. For example, a model might represent clouds in just two ways: Over any given location on the imaginary earth, clouds either exist or do not exist. They are either "on" or "off," like a light switch. The computer is programmed to throw the switch based on the amount of moisture present in the simulated atmosphere. This is a very simplified and streamlined way for a computer to represent clouds. But it saves time.

Another limitation of climate models is in their resolution, a term we encountered in our discussion of the efforts of Lewis Fry Richardson in the early twentieth century. In order to get a perfectly accurate forecast, a computer would have to simulate the motions of every single air molecule in the atmosphere. This is impossible. Climate models, therefore, divide the earth up into a grid and predict the weather only at the grid points. The models also divide the atmosphere up into horizontal layers, stacked like the layers of a cake. In a typical climate model, grid points might be spaced 100 miles apart and there might be anywhere from two to thirty layers. Dividing the earth and the atmosphere up like this significantly reduces the amount of work that the computer has to do and allows it to calculate future climate in a relatively short period of time.

The distance between the grid points and between the layers is called the model's resolution. The resolution of a climate model is like the accuracy of a person's vision. A low, or coarse, resolution is like having blurry eyesight—you can make out general forms and figures, but the details are missing. When a climate model has a relatively coarse resolution, it might do well predicting the big picture, such as large-scale trends of temperature over a continent, but it won't be able to predict details, such as the way rainfall and temperature vary over a single mountain range. This is important because the overall weather of the planet is shaped in part by what goes on in the atmosphere over relatively small areas. Since a climate model can't take into account the weather conditions in between its grid points, it may be missing some potentially significant data and will turn out a less accurate forecast. Leave out the garlic, and you still have a meal, but it's not as good as it could have been.

The resolution of a climate model is related to the amount of number crunching the model must do and the speed of the supercomputer. The faster the supercomputer and the simpler the climate model, the higher the resolution it can have. However, the simpler the climate model, the more shortcuts it must take in simulating the various natural processes that affect climate. The more shortcuts, the less accurate the model. Scientists try to overcome these difficulties by running complex models with a high, or fine, resolution but programming them to simulate the climate only over a small portion of the earth. They can then see how the future climate may change on a regional scale. To observe climate changes on a global scale, scientists must use simpler models with a relatively coarse resolution.

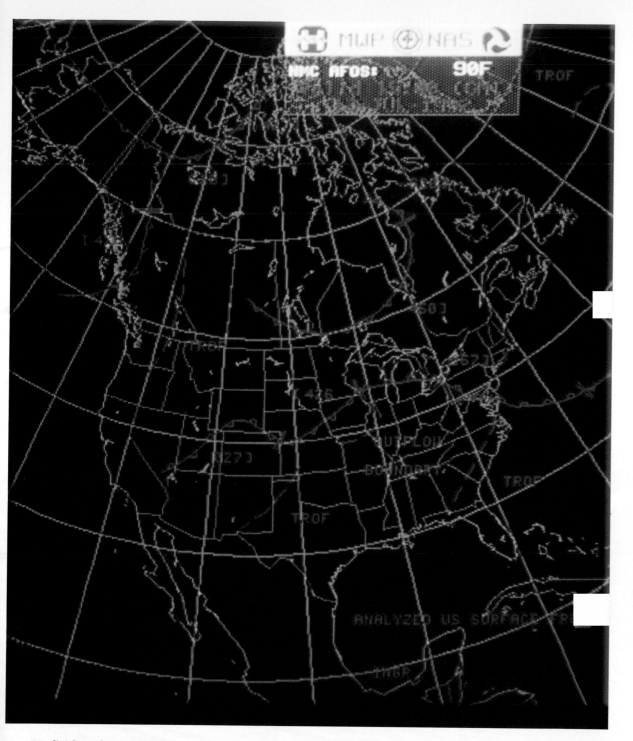

By dividing the earth into a grid and predicting the weather only at grid points, climate models allow computers to calculate future climate with surprising accuracy.

A climate model with a relatively coarse resolution may not be able to predict the way rainfall varies in a locale between grid points.

Another limitation of computer models lies in their sensitivity to initial conditions. Initial conditions, remember, are the numbers that represent the state of the atmosphere at a beginning point in time. Scientists have found that if you change the initial conditions in a computer model by just a little bit, you can wind up with a drastically different forecast. This is one of the reasons why it's so difficult to predict the weather beyond several days in advance. Long-term climate models, however, are less sensitive to initial conditions because these climate models are less concerned with details and more focused on general trends over long periods of time.

In summary, climate models come with important built-in limitations. These limitations are the result of our imperfect understanding of the natural world, the speed limit of our supercomputers, and the complexity of the atmosphere. As computer technology gets better, climate models will make more accurate predictions. Already, the most advanced climate models have shown impressive agreement about the future of the earth's climate. In the next chapter, we'll learn about the answers that climate models have provided to the following question: How will the earth's climate change as a result of rising levels of greenhouse gases?

4 The Forecast

There are a variety of different computer models that researchers can use to predict future climate. The kind of model that scientists use depends on what they want to study. Some climate models are complex and detailed but calculate the climate only over certain regions of the world. Others are simplified and may predict how changing the amount of carbon dioxide in the air will affect temperatures and sea levels around the earth decades into the future, but leave out predictions of rainfall. Some models focus only on a certain kind of natural phenomenon, such as the role of plants and trees in regulating the amount of carbon dioxide in the air. A climate model might be programmed to just simulate the ocean with its complicated currents. A common procedure is for scientists to take two computer

Scientists agree that preserving forests around the world will be beneficial to the earth's future climate.

models, one that simulates the ocean and one that simulates the atmosphere, and link them up together to see how they interact. In these kinds of "coupled" ocean-atmosphere models, scientists pay particular attention to how the computer simulates the exchange of heat and moisture between the air and the water.

Climate models require some special care to ensure that the calculations they produce are as correct as possible. When scientists hit the "start" button on a computer model, they often set the imaginary date 100 or more years into the past. This is because the start of a computerized climate simulation often does not match reality right away. Part of the reason for this is because of the basic limitations of the climate model, such as resolution and parameterization. The climate model is therefore programmed to simulate year after year of the earth's climate through history, allowing it to become more and more stable over time. A climate model becomes stable when its simulated version of the climate matches the actual climate that exists today. Scientists refer to this process as spin up.

Scientists have encountered a problem with spin up. Often, when a model simulates year after year of historical climate, it begins to drift away from an accurate representation of the atmosphere. The phenomenon is like the drift of a car to one side of the road after you let go of the steering wheel. When scientists start a climate model and let it run by itself for a while, it often drifts into an unnaturally warm climate scenario. Researchers often have to use something called flux adjustments to try to nudge the climate model back into line. A flux adjustment is basically a fudge factor. It's just a way of changing some of the parameters in a model so that by the time the model has completed its spin up, its simulated climate matches the earth's actual climate. But the use of flux adjustments has cast some doubt over the overall accuracy of climate models. After all, how can people rely on climate model predictions when scientists must artificially nudge the model to fit reality? Others argue that the question is irrelevant, since the only thing that matters is the prediction of the model once it has spun up and is in agreement with the observed climate. And, recently, computer programmers have started to develop climate models that do not need flux adjustments, spinning up into a more or less accurate version of global climate without any help.

Another challenge that climate models encounter after scientists hit the start button is something called feedback. Feedback occurs when two or more processes affect one another in a chain of cause and effect. Positive feedback occurs when the processes act to enhance one another, while negative feedback occurs when the processes act to weaken one another.

We've already touched on a couple of feedback processes earlier in this book. Polar ice, for example, can have a positive feedback on the earth's climate. A warming planet will melt more and more polar ice, allowing less sunlight to reflect back into space and more sunlight to be absorbed by the earth. The more sunlight absorbed by the

Higher temperatures from global warming will mean a higher rate of water evaporation from oceans and lakes and, therefore, more water vapor, which is a greenhouse gas, in the atmosphere.

earth, the warmer it becomes, and the warmer it becomes, the more polar ice melts.

Clouds can have a negative feedback on climate. If global warming continues on its present course, more water will evaporate from the oceans into the air, causing the atmosphere to become more humid. The higher the humidity in the atmosphere, the more clouds form. The more clouds there are, the less sunlight is able to reach the surface of the earth and the cooler it becomes.

Water vapor can have a positive feedback on climate. Water vapor is just the invisible, gaseous form of water and is produced through the process of evaporation. The amount of water vapor in the air depends in part on the air temperature: The higher the temperature, the more water evaporates from oceans and lakes and the more water vapor is able to collect in the atmosphere. But like carbon dioxide, water vapor is a greenhouse gas, so the greater the amount of water vapor in the atmosphere, the warmer the earth may become. The warmer the earth, the higher the rate of evaporation and the more water vapor collects in the air.

Plants can have a negative feedback on climate, at least to a point. Plants absorb carbon dioxide from the atmosphere in the process of photosynthesis, which generates plant-building material and releases oxygen into the air. The more carbon dioxide there is in the atmosphere, the more efficiently plants are able to grow and ingest carbon dioxide. Therefore, increasing levels of atmospheric carbon dioxide are somewhat restricted as growing plants absorb more carbon dioxide from the air. But scientists studying the behavior of plants think that there's a limit to just how much carbon dioxide plants can absorb.

Climate models, therefore, must meet the challenges of spin up, flux adjustment, and feedback mechanisms, as well as the built-in limitations of models, such as resolution and parameterization. Despite all these challenges, the best, most detailed climate models of today have come to similar conclusions about the future of the earth's climate. These forecasts are based on a doubling of the amount of carbon dioxide in the atmosphere through the twenty-first century.

All climate models predict an increase in the average temperature of the earth. In general, they predict that the average temperature of the earth will rise anywhere from three to nearly eleven degrees Fahrenheit. The predicted global warming in the coming decades, however, does not occur evenly over the planet. Some locations warm more than others, while some parts of the world even cool slightly. For instance, climate models generally predict greater warming of the air over land as compared to over oceans. This is mostly because oceans have a greater ability to absorb and hold heat than land, so it takes longer exposure to higher air temperatures for them to warm up. Furthermore, the global warming predicted by climate models is greatest in the winter and at high latitudes—closer to the North and South Poles. This regional variation in temperature change is thought to be the result of less snow and the melting of polar ice caps in a warmer world. By contrast, most models do not predict much temperature change in tropical regions. Worldwide, nighttime temperatures may become higher on average than daytime temperatures, in part because of a forecasted increase in the amount of cloudiness. Clouds affect temperature by absorbing radiation emitted by the earth. Since this radiation would otherwise escape into space, the atmosphere remains warmer at night when clouds are overhead.

Climate models also generally predict an increase in the amount of precipitation around the earth. Precipitation is just a scientific term for rain, snow, and anything else that falls from the clouds. Just as with the predicted increase in temperatures, however, the predicted increase in precipitation does not occur evenly over the entire planet. The models seem to suggest that rain and snow will

Climate models predict that global warming will have the most impact during winter and in the North and South Poles, resulting in the melting of polar ice caps.

increase more during the winter than during the summer. During the summer, more of the rain that falls will be from thunderstorms, rather than from steady, light rain.

Computer models also predict an increased threat for drought in some parts of the world. This may seem strange, since they also predict a global increase in the amount of rain and snow. The answer to this seeming contradiction lies in the process of evaporation. The higher the temperature, the higher the rate of evaporation. Moisture evaporating from the ground dries the land out, so in a warmer world, droughts may start earlier, last longer, and become more severe. Computer models suggest this will be especially true in regions of the world that are already relatively dry, such as grasslands adjacent to deserts. But the threat of floods may rise for the same reason. The higher the rate of evaporation, the more water vapor is able to build up in the atmosphere. The amount of rain that can fall from a cloud partially depends on how much water vapor is available in the atmosphere. So in a warmer, more humid world, when the storms do come, they may unleash a torrent of flooding rainfall.

Finally, most advanced climate models are programmed to predict the changes in sea levels that result from global warming. Sea levels rise as warmer air temperatures melt polar ice caps, and as ocean water molecules expand as water temperatures rise. Climate models estimate that sea levels may rise anywhere from 5.5 inches to over 32 inches by the year 2100. While coastal cities such as New York and San

Although global temperatures are expected to rise, scientists predict a global increase in rain and snow as a result of global warming.

Francisco won't be flooded outright by a thirty-inch rise in ocean water, this kind of water rise will significantly add to the destructive effects of coastal storms. Pounding waves and currents will cause much more damage to beachfront property.

Though the forecasts from climate models are in remarkable agreement, different models can end up with different future climate scenarios because each climate model is programmed slightly differently. For example, there are various ways that scientists can use parameterization for certain natural processes. Some climate researchers might prefer to leave certain natural processes out of their models completely, while other researchers may decide to include them. But the consistency that various climate models have shown in their results allows scientists to become more confident in their predictive powers. Lewis Fry Richardson wrote in 1922 of his painstaking efforts in forecasting weather, "Perhaps some day in the dim future it will be possible to advance the computations faster than the weather advances . . . but that is a dream." Today, Richardson's dream has become reality.

Conclusion

From Isaac Newton's seventeenth century mathematical revolution, to Lewis Fry Richardson's laborious calculations in the early twentieth century, to the powerful supercomputers of the present day, the effort to predict future climate is one of science's greatest endeavors. As it becomes clearer that humans have begun to influence the natural balance of the planet, we try to understand how our actions may change the earth's climate. The task is extremely difficult, as the earth's atmosphere is directly linked to the oceans, polar ice caps, plants and trees, and a variety of other natural phenomena. Using supercomputers, scientists try to forecast the future and predict the effects of increasing greenhouse gas levels. The limits of our ability to forecast the climate are tied to the limits of our tools. Sophisticated as they are, computers aren't able to come close to simulating the level of complexity in the natural world. Using our still incomplete understanding of the earth, the atmosphere, and the

Computer models suggest that regions of the world that are already relatively dry, such as grasslands adjacent to deserts, will face an increased threat of drought.

oceans, scientists program climate models to the best of their present ability. But as the available tools improve, predictions will become more and more accurate. The agreement in the output of various computer models, run by different groups of researchers all over the world, lends even more credibility to the vision of a warmer planet in the decades ahead. It seems increasingly likely, based on current trends and forecasts from climate models, that the rising levels of greenhouse gases in the earth's atmosphere will bring about major changes in the global climate in the twenty-first century.

Glossary

aerosols Tiny, airborne particles created from industrial pollutants. Aerosols have a cooling effect on the atmosphere by reflecting sunlight back into space.

biome A community of plants and animals living in a common natural environment. Examples of biomes include rain forest, grassland, desert, and tundra.

climate The average weather conditions over a long period of time, generally decades or more.

climate model Complex computer software that simulates the atmosphere and sometimes other natural phenomena like oceans and plants. These models are run on large super-computers and predict how the climate might change as a result of increasing greenhouse gases in the atmosphere.

evaporation The process whereby liquid water changes into invisible, gaseous water vapor.

feedback The phenomenon in which two processes or events influence one another. Feedback can be negative, in which case the two processes act to cancel one another out, or positive, in which case the processes act to enhance one another.

flux adjustment A method of "nudging" a climate model into a realistic representation of the atmosphere.

fossil fuel Any fuel made from the decayed remains of ancient plant life; includes coal, natural gas, and oil. Fossil fuels take millions of years to create.

global warming The warming of the planet due to increasing amounts of greenhouse gases in the atmosphere.

greenhouse gas Any gas that efficiently absorbs outgoing radiation from the earth, thereby contributing to global warming. The main greenhouse gases are water vapor, carbon dioxide, methane, nitrous oxide, chlorofluorocarbons, and ozone.

grid A checkerboard-like pattern of points laid out on a computerized representation of the earth. Climate models predict weather conditions only at the grid points, thus saving time.

initial conditions A set of data that represents a "snapshot" of the weather in time. Computer models predict future climate by using initial conditions as input for mathematical equations. These equations then calculate how the atmosphere will change over time.

parameterization A shortcut in computer models, whereby complex natural processes are represented in a very simple way. Parameterization saves time in calculating future climate.

photosynthesis   The process whereby plants use sunlight to convert carbon dioxide and water into plant-building materials.

radiation   Energy in the form of invisible electromagnetic waves that travel at the speed of light.

resolution   The distance between grid points in a computer model. The finer the resolution of a grid, the more detail the model can predict.

spin up   The process by which computer models simulate the atmosphere through history in order to reach a realistic representation of the climate.

supercomputer   A large and extremely powerful computer that can be used by scientists to simulate and predict the earth's climate.

For More Information

American Meteorological Society (AMS)
45 Beacon Street
Boston, MA 02108-3693
Web site: http://www.ametsoc.org/AMS
The AMS is the premiere professional
meteorological organization in the
United States.

Geophysical Fluid Dynamics
Laboratory/National Oceanic and
Atmospheric Administration
P.O. Box 308
Princeton, NJ 08542-0308
(609) 452-6500
Web site: http://www.gfdl.gov

The Geophysical Fluid Dynamics Laboratory (GFDL) is one of the premiere climate research organizations in the world. The GFDL uses state-of-the-art computer models to predict how greenhouse gases may influence climate.

Intergovernmental Panel on Climate Change (IPCC)
c/o World Meteorological Organization
7 bis Avenue de la Paix
C.P. 2300
CH-1211 Geneva 2
Switzerland
Web site: http://www.ipcc.ch
From its Web site, you can download the same IPCC reports consulted by governments worldwide.

Weatherwise Magazine
Heldref Publications
1319 Eighteenth Street NW
Washington, DC 20036-1802
(202) 296-6267
Web site: http://www.weatherwise.org
A popular magazine about all things weather. Find it at your local library or newsstand.

For Further Reading

Carr, Michael William. *Weather Predicting Simplified*. New York: McGraw Hill, 1999.

Hodgson, Michael. *Weather Forecasting*. 2nd ed. Globe Pequot Press, 1999.

Stevens, William K. *The Change in the Weather: People, Weather, and the Science of Climate*. New York: Delacorte Press, 1999.

Weiss, Ann E. *Seers and Scientists: Can the Future Be Predicted?* San Diego: Harcourt Brace, 1986.

Index

About the Author

Paul Stein has a B.S. in meteorology from Pennsylvania State University. He has eight years experience as a weather forecaster, most recently as a senior meteorologist for the Weather Channel. Currently, he develops computer systems and software that display and process weather-related data.

Photo Credits

Cover © Artville Weatherstock: storm clouds.

Cover inset © Scientific Visualization Studio, NASA/GSFC: Hurricane Floyd effects on coastal ecology.

Front and back matter © Ross M. Horowitz/Image Bank: rain.

Introduction background © Image Bank: Alaska.

Chapter 1 background © Wallace Garrison/Index Stock: close-up of drought-stricken earth.

Chapter 2 background © Vic Bider/Index Stock: snow in Chicago, Illinois.

Chapter 3 background © Bill Bachmann/Photo Researchers, Inc.: flooded land.

Series Design and Layout

Geri Giordano